six nights on the hook at
SANTA CRUZ ISLAND

six nights on the hook at
SANTA CRUZ ISLAND

JAMES FREDERICK

Copyright © 2019 James Frederick

All rights reserved. This book or parts thereof may not be reproduced in any form, stored in any retrieval system, or transmitted in any form by any means—electronic, mechanical, photocopy, recording, or otherwise—without prior written permission of the publisher, except as provided by United States of America copyright law. For permission requests, write to the publisher, at jamesthesailorman@gmail.com

Edited by Camille Schefter and Kate Harding

Design and Layout by James Frederick

Self Published through Ingram Sparks
First Printed, 2019

ISBN: 978-0-9824008-6-9

svtriteia.com

Thanks to my mama,
I wish you knew me now.

&

Thanks to my wife Camille,
For knowing me better
Than I know myself

CONTENTS

FOREWORD..9

INTRODUCTION..16

DEPARTURE..25

COCHES PRIETOS....................................41

MORSE POINT...55

FORNEY COVE...71

CUEVA VALDEZ..85

PELICAN BAY..99

LITTLE SCORPION.................................113

LINKS...131

AFTERWORD..133

FORE

It has been a while since I have read an authors work whom extolled the virtues of taking a sailboat cruising on a small budget. The video blogs and instagram posts, which dominate the mediation of exploring on a small sailboat in the late part of the second decade of the twenty first century, paint a picture of a lifestyle. Even what is left of the sailing print media mostly portray the cruising sailor as someone whom divides their time between yoga poses, developing fine fusion cuisine, outfitting a boat in the digital age, and pontificating over a great sunset or sunrise. Don't get me wrong, I imbibe in all of these pass times and I see the virtues in them. But, there is a division between the picture contemporary mediation of the cruising sailor paints of why and how we go to sea and the picture painted by the earlier generations. Sterling Hayden famously said, " To be truly challenging, a voyage, like a life, must rest on a firm foundation of financial unrest. Otherwise you are doomed to a routine traverse, the kind known to yachtsmen, who play with their boats at sea." It seems to me that the change in how and why we decide to go to sea is dictated by who is telling us the story. In the books of the Roths, the Pardeys, or even Slocum, the cruising sailor takes on voyaging as a vocation, not a lifestyle. Seamanship is a body of skills, which have to be studied, learned and executed by the mariner. Like Harlan and Anna Hubbard's move onto a shanty boat on the Ohio River after World War 2, the cruising sailor of the past had manufactured a new career as a voyager, which existed for the most part, outside of the mainstream economy. And like the Hubbards several of these voyagers shared their experiences on paper.

James Frederick is a mariner of the older cannon. He is an autodidact who has studied seamanship with the same attention to detail a machinist studies their trade. James shares his process of apprenticeship with the sea in the media platforms that dominate, instagram and YouTube. What James describes in his photos, videos, and writing is the story of a journeyman cruising sailor learning their craft. It is honest, insightful, and attainable. The choices James makes demonstrate that a life at sea does not depend on a lot of money. He also describes, that, like any life on this planet, it does require some money. However, James clarifies that investing in a boat and gear is a lot like any investment, it will yield a far better result if the decisions are made with a careful analysis of the market. But Frederick's goal is not to yield financial gain from his labor and expenditures, but to develop his craft. It is no coincidence that Frederick is an artist, a vocation long inhabited by people who practiced their trade in the service of culture rather than for personal financial gain. Frederick's work is a representation of what is possible when someone ceases thinking of themselves as a worker in so far as how much money they can yield but instead, a worker in producing the life which they find meaningful.

Captain Noah Peffer
Los Angeles, October 2019

Captain Peffer grew up sailing the East Coast and Bahamas on the David Stevens schooner Sarah Abbott (sister ship to Atlantas!) with his family. He is an Artist, Carpenter, Educator and Sailor. Peffer was Professor and Captain at the University of Southern California in Nautical Sciences. Currently Noah and his wife Al are crusing full-time in Mexico on their refit J42, SV Thylacine.

THE ALBERG 30

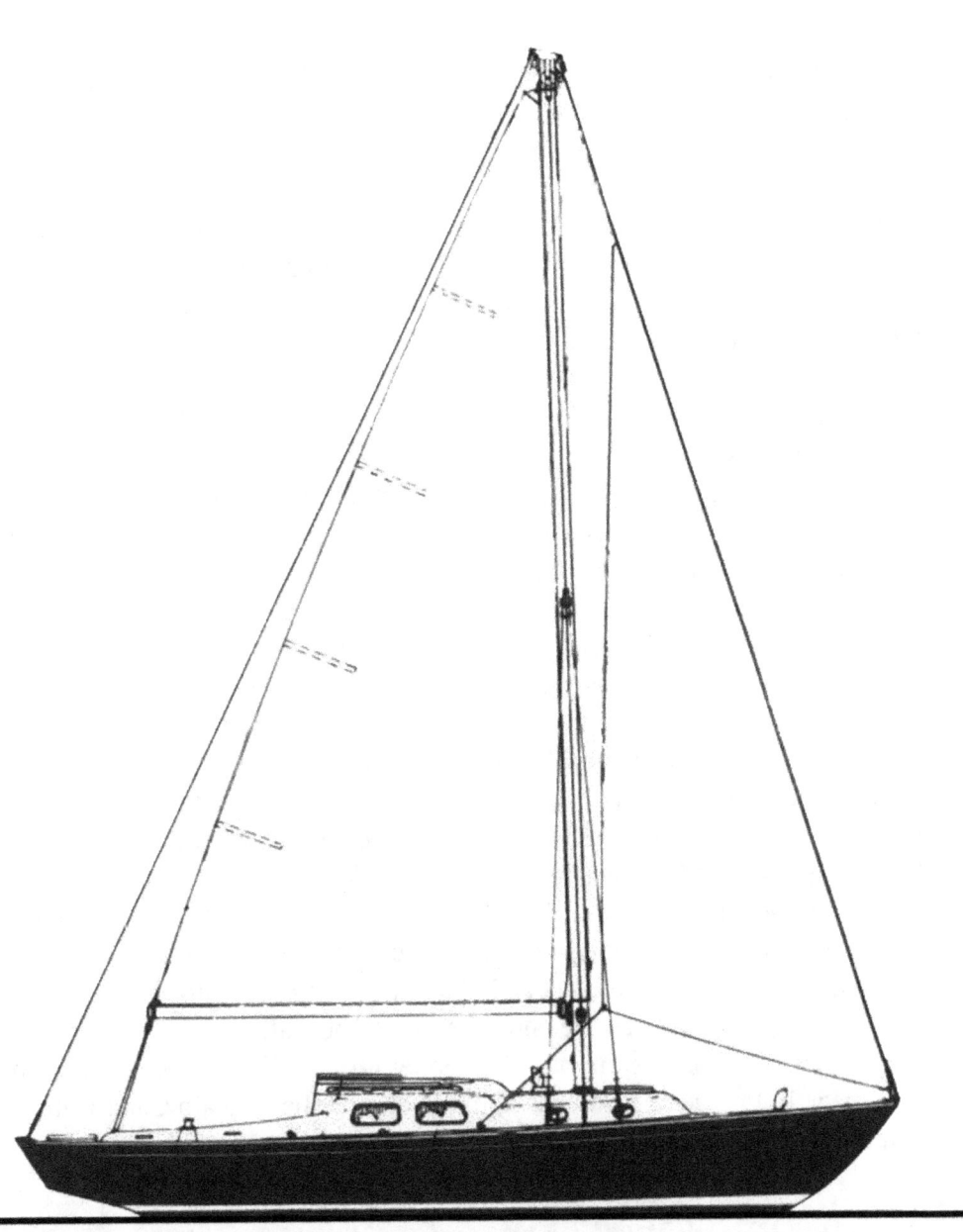

INTRODUCTION

Call me Sailor James.

Some years ago - never mind how long precisely – having little or no money in my purse, I was pursuing a career in fine art and in this pursuit I found myself on the island of Kotlin, off the coast of Saint Petersburg, Russia. I had been invited by the National Center for Contemporary Arts Saint Petersburg to spend time there making art and presenting an exhibition in Kronstadt. The city and the island have a rich maritime history. The flat I was staying in was directly behind an incredible Naval Cathedral and the building directly in front of the studio was a hundred year old sailmaker's loft for a hundred years. During that residency I dove into all things maritime and tried to learn everything I could about the ancient culture that is sailing. I studied the history of the compass, I documented all of the lighthouses I could, made paintings based on the shapes of sails, and completed a body of work that I exhibited both in Russia and in Los Angeles upon my return to the states. I was rabid to know more about all things sailing related.

Soon an opportunity came up to travel to Scotland and make art on a 52-foot sailboat as part of another artist residency. I was already writing for the Huffington Post about my time in Russia and the artwork I created there so I continued writing for them about my travels in Scotland in the form of journals and essays.

The program combined artists, scientists and sailors to see what would come of the pairings and for each of the individuals to be inspired and influenced by one another. For my part of the residence I designed and built a "Drawing Machine" that used a fixed pen mounted above a wheeled drawing platter. My intention was to allow the boat's movements at sea to create drawings or make marks on the paper I had prepared for the residency. This was in the month of September in the year two thousand and fourteen.

Arriving in Scotland I had read everything I could about the Orkney Islands, their history, and about sailing and exploring under sail. The moment I stepped onboard SY Selkie my life changed forever. I remember looking at the boat from across the dock wondering what all the lines did, wondering how such a "heavy" looking boat could sail with any efficiency, knowing nothing of hull shape or the concept of displacement. Once onboard my eyes darted madly as I tried to take in my new surroundings, wanting to see every detail at once and make sense of it all.

Selkie was a custom built 52-foot aluminum lifting keel sailboat that was made in France and purchased in Croatia by the Captain Celia Bull. The Captain and her son had lived aboard for the last 10 years.

The Captain was very patient and supportive with me as I was desperate to learn everything I could about sailing. She had been captaining these artists and scientist residencies all summer and said she was happy to have someone on board that actually wanted to learn how to sail. She taught me how to plot our course on paper, how to check the extreme tides in the UK, I learned to helm under motor and sail, we anchored almost every night and I was stationed at the bow during anchoring and hauling up.

Celia had been one of the United Kingdom's top female mountain climbers until she was climbing a sea stack in Tasmania and a boulder the size of TV came loose and struck her boyfriend and climbing partner. She hoisted his alive but limp body up to a ledge and secured him before climbing down and running for miles for aid. After the accident and time spent nursing him back to the best of health she could, Celia quit climbing entirely and began sailing. Before long she was working as a deckhand on a large sailing vessel taking documentary film crews between Chile, Antarctica and 60 foot seas in Southern Ocean on passage to the South Georgia Islands.

During our time sailing in Orkney we visited a total of seven islands including the isle of North Ronaldsay where we got to see the The semi-feral flock of North Ronaldsay Sheep who are believed to have been brought to the island by neolithic man some 5000 years ago. While the harsh environment drove early man away the sheep remained and evolved to survive on eating seaweed. The only land animal, apart from the marine iguana in the Galapagos, known to survive on such a diet. The Island of North Ronaldsay is featured in the Viking Sagas as a location of a great battle between Earls resulting in a "Blood Eagle" of one of the Earls.

The Orkney Islands are rich with history that moved me in ways I can't explain. These harsh barren lands sitting exposed to the elements that we had traveled to in the same manner as our ancestors before us. This sense of time travel took hold of me and has yet to let go.

All but two of the other passengers disembarked at Stromness, myself and one other artist. I was asked if I wanted to stay on as crew and help return the boat to the island of Eigg , Selkie's home port. I instantly agreed and soon we were off sailing through Pentland Firth, down the North Sea to Inverness where we entered the Caledonian Canal. Transiting the Canal took us across Loch Ness and through the Highlands of Scotland. I disembarked at Neptune's Staircase and took a train to Glasgow to fly home. My life had a new purpose: to sail.

I have an unquenchable thirst for knowledge and I'm a very passionate person. The magic of traveling under sail to new islands each day and exploring lands with ancient histories had derailed my life in the most incredible way. Upon returning home to Los Angeles I realized I had no interest in an art career and that all I wanted to do was to be sailing. I could think of nothing else and started trying to figure out how to get on boats in Los

Angeles and dreaming up ways I could somehow get my own. I still continued showing artwork, and had some of my work go viral online, which lead to a lot of sales. I would squirrel money away when I could for my boat fund and save what I could from my job. I work as a freelance arthandler, installing art in some of the biggest galleries in the world and in the homes of countless celebrities in Los Angeles. This type of job afforded me the possibility to take time off for the artist's residencies that led me to sailing...but life always had a way of sneaking up on me and keeping my savings too low for the type of boat I dreamt of having.

I finally found my way onto boats in Southern California by signing up for "Meet Up" groups that offered day sails for a $20 donation. I went on every day sail I could get on through the website and made friends with one of the captains, Mark Wilson. I am not a competitive person, and racing never really interested me before, but any chance to be on the water and I was there. Mark invited me to crew on his 38 ft Catalina for a Wednesday night beer can race and soon I was racing on his boat as well as a Santana 30/30 on Tuesday nights. I always tell anyone that says they want to learn how to sail to get on a Corinthian racing team. You'll learn far more about how to sail from racing than you will during a 1000 day sails.

In 2015 I had also signed up on every sailor placement website I could find, and that June I was invited to crew onboard a delivery from San Diego to the San Francisco Bay. It wasn't a paid position but all the provisions would be covered and, more importantly, I would get time on a delivery covering a large distance. The boat was the famous Islander 36, Intrepid, which Zac Suderland had circumnavigated in in 2004. The boat was owned by Tim Brill at the time I was on board (Tim is still sailing Intrepid and more than half way through his circumnavigation). On this trip I started documenting my sailing adventures and uploading them to YouTube. I had watched every single episode of "Distant Horizons" on pay-per-view and was regularly watching the few channels that existed on YouTube in 2015. This was long before Patreon and the hundreds of sailing channels that now populate the site. I was too shy to talk on camera and wasn't comfortable filming the interactions of the other crew members, so my earliest episodes were not that interesting and mostly consisted of beautiful visuals with good music. I did write extensive journals on my blog and felt the videos were like a support document for the journals. Something I learned for certain about this trip was that I was not interested in making a habit of sailing up the coast of California. Traveling against the currents and the Northerlies that are a constant on the coast makes for lots of very slow motoring and very uncomfortable conditions. I did learn a lot on that delivery and was getting much needed time at sea.

The next year through a similar site I was hired to crew onboard a

42ft Dufor that needed to be sailed from Puerto Rico to North Carolina. After 5 days at sea in the middle of the notorious Bermuda Triangle our weather routing service contacted us and told us if we couldn't make landfall on the mainland within 24 hours we had to run for Bermuda. There was a massive storm barreling out of the Chesapeake Bay heading right for us. The captain changed course, emailed our families, and we sailed at between 10 -12 knots to Bermuda with a lifeless engine and a scrambled autopilot that held course, but without a legible display. The famous Newport to Bermuda Race was also happening at the same time and a large number of boats dropped out due to the 40+ knots that came with this system. This was great luck for me because it gave me the chance to sail to Bermuda! After we spent a day in Bermuda and rode out the storm, which hit hours after we arrived and tied up we pushed off and headed for the Outer Banks of North Carolina.

By 2017 I had earned a lot of sea miles, blue water passages and a wealth of experience in sailing. I had been sharing a 26' Excalibur with my friend Neil Fletcher in Marina del Rey, gotten my first trip to Catalina under my belt, and was still looking for my own boat.

The apartment I had been living in for the last 16 years was the bottom half of a hundred year old house in Los Angeles' quickly changing Echo Park neighborhood. My landlord had passed away in his 90s and his widow sold the house in probate. The new owners, thanks to very strict California renters rights, had to pay me $18,000 to move out. This was the windfall of cash I had needed to buy my dreamboat.

After moving expenses I had about 14,000 in my boat budget. I had been looking at boats all over the world for months but refused to by one that I felt I was settling for or that deviated from my strict list of requirements.

- Must be made before 1972
- Must have a solid hull (no core)
- Must be a bluewater boat with Full Keel or Skeg hung rudder
- Preferably have a tiller
- Preferably have a head or room for one
- Preferably have a diesel engine

Everything else I knew I could work out later. I did see tons of incredible blue water boats, but they were all much more expensive than the $14,000 I had in my budget. I had read "Twenty Small Sailboats to Take You Anywhere" over and over, and my top 3 were a Pearson Triton 28, Westsail 32 and the Alberg 30. I obsessively watched craigslist up and down the west coast, and even in Florida. At one point I almost bought an early number Triton in Chicago. I was also looking at a number of Tartan 34s but

I didn't like that they have lifting centerboards. At one point I came very close to buying a Triton but had held back because the inboard had been removed and the propshaft hole had been glassed over.

Then on April 28th 2017 I saw a listing for a 1965 Alberg 30 right here in Los Angeles and they were only asking $2500. I immediately contacted the seller and arranged to see it the next day. I remember driving down to Wilmington, near Long Beach to see the boat, cash in my pocket, and sick to my stomach with anxiety about the whole situation. I was so close to having a large part of my dreams coming true; it was very stressful. Arriving at the boat I looked over it with the owner, Stefan, as we looked in all the nooks and crannies he explained that the engine was seized or non-functional, I knew the boat was thick hand laid fiberglass and that it was built like a tank. I could see slight delamination on the mast beam which was a known weakness of these boats, along with the chain plate bolts sizing being too small. The rig looked good, all of the systems had been taken out or stolen from the boat, but the boat itself was solid and the only softspots on the topsides were in the cockpit. The deck itself was solid everywhere I tapped and walked. Without hesitation I told him I would buy the boat if they would transfer the slip to me. He seemed shocked and we went up to the marina office. They transferred the slip to me and we did the paperwork. I knew what this boat was worth and what she would be worth with a little work so I did not try and negotiate the price and I agreed to pay the full $2500. Stefan was so confused that I didn't try to haggle him he gave me a $100 back when I handed him the money. So there I was, I had just bought my dreamboat for $2400.

Now, I have been called a lot of things in my life but lazy was never one of them. My brothers and myself were raised by a very strict mother who believed in hard work She taught us the importance of a good work ethic and administered her fair share of tough love. Being made to work hard as a child has actually made my life easier, I can work very long hours, don't allow myself to cut corners or do things the easy way if it means the outcome will suffer. This aspect of my upbringing really paid off, considering I had just bought a boat that needed a complete refit. The work began immediately and within a few weeks I found a beautifully rebuilt Yanmar 2GM20f to replace the seized Yanmar 2GM20 that came with the boat.

Buying the boat also meant it was time to really get serious about my YouTube channel. I began filming everything I could. From the purchase of the boat to the countless major projects that I dove into once she was mine. Filming myself pulling out the old engine, diving on the bottom for the first time with my brother Colby, installing the new engine and my first sail on my own boat, SV Trietia. All of this took place in a two month time frame.

After I got her sailing and did my first trip to Catalina Island in

August I got right back to work on projects preparing her for my dream trip: spending Christmas and New Years at the Channel Islands. I had dreamt of sailing to the Channel Islands since returning from Orkney. They are far more wild than Catalina Island and to spend time there you must have adequate ground tackle and an understanding of what can happen if the Santa Anas show up with you on a lee shore (more about the Santa Anas in Chapter 1).

I had tried to figure out a way to sail to the islands for Christmas the last two years but the boats I had access to didn't have reliable anchor setups that could be trusted for anchoring at the Channel Islands, and I certainly couldn't afford a charter there.

This year I was finally going to make it happen no matter what.

Which brings us up to date for the book you are about to read. Six Nights on the Hook at Santa Cruz Island is a collection of my journals from that trip and my thoughts and feelings after it was all said and done. I keep written journals and logs for all of my sailing adventures and I have written this book using those journals, logs, videos, and podcasts I recorded at each of the six anchorages I visited on the island.

One of my motivations for writing this book was to record a moment in my life that was of great importance to me. A simple story about what some might consider a simple trip. There are countless books about crossing oceans by sail or rounding the horn, I know because I've read every single one I can get my hands on. But this book is about something smaller in scale. Something possibly routine for the local sailors of Ventura, Oxnard and Santa Barbara whom casually hop over to the islands for long weekends.

I think of these small sailing trips that we fit into our lives as "lower-case sailing". It's something that is possible for sailors on a budget to manage and make happen. It is an achievable goal once you have a boat and the right equipment needed. One could do the same trip I describe in this book on a much smaller boat than Trietia. It is about what is within our reach. Sometimes you will find that short trips to local islands or anchorages is exactly what you need to be happy and satisfied, which is a beautiful thing. Others of us will find that the exhilaration of "destination sailing" encourages us to go a little further each time and equip our boat a little more, always pursuing that next anchorage, near or far.

So this is my simple story, of one of the best weeks of my entire life.

James Frederick,
Los Angeles, 2019

- CHAPTER 1 -

The passage to
**Coches Prietos Anchorage
Santa Cruz Island**

77 nm | 22.5 hours | Motorsail

December 23 2017
33°45'52"N 118°15'03"W

    I was laying cramped and crooked in my port lazarette alternating between a battle with my packing nut and having a full on meltdown complete with cursing, kicking and punching the fiberglass hole I was currently wedged into. The packing nut, which is basically a collar that keeps the sea out of the boat while also allowing the propeller shaft to spin, was leaking quite a bit more than I was comfortable with and I was suppose to have already left the dock for my long over night passage to Santa Cruz Island of the Channel Islands of California. The only access to the packing nut is through a small bronze hole in the cockpit or a larger opening inside the lazarette, and by larger I mean a 6" x 10" access door that I can only get one arm into at a time. The port lazarette and myself are very well acquainted as I had spent countless hours inside the tight quarters while installing my engine and waterlift earlier in the year. Now I was an hour past my planned departure time and I thought I would just climb in and give the packing nut a tightening to slow down the drip, which is common procedure with this type of stuffing box. But I couldn't for the life of me get the lock nut on the packing nut to "break" which is required to retighten the whole business.

    Leading up to this moment was a whirlwind of very long days and monumental projects on the boat. I somehow managed to pull them off but at a cost to my physical and mental state, which was becoming apparent as I struggled. For the last two months I had built a custom chain locker, installed a manual windlass, bow roller, anchor and 680' of anchor rode (80' of 3/8 BBB chain and 600' of rope rode). I had also cut all of the cabinetry out of my head, installed a holding tank and a new cabinet and all new plumbing. I removed the old icebox in the cabin and replaced it with a temporary chart table and navigation station. All of this took place on the weekends and after I got off of work from my day job each weeknight. Week after week I would work until 6pm then make the 35-minute drive to the boat then work until 10 or 11pm and head home to repeat the process.

    The weeks of exhaustion had finally caught up with me, as I lay frustrated and upset inside the portside lazarette. I was finally able to get the locknut broken free with the help of my girlfriend at the time, Meital, whom had spent almost as much time on the boat as I had during the first few months of my stewardship. We had done this same routine originally when I installed the beautifully rebuilt Yanmar 2GM20f in July. Meital would lay in the cockpit and reach through the 6" bronze access hole holding one wrench steady while I was inside the lazarette pushing the other wrench. It took us over an hour to get it broken free the first time we did this. The main difference was that the waterlift had been installed and was directly above the packing nut making it almost impossible to work on it.

I finally managed to get it broken free and tightened it up as best I could, slowing the drip, drip, drip some but not as much as I would have liked. I decided to keep an eye on it and the level of water in the bilge for the next several hours and if it seemed to be an issue I would pull into Marina Del Rey at first light and repack the packing nut. I had all of the materials onboard to do so if need be.

I untied from the dock at 16:30, two hours later than my planned departure time. Meital and my friend Christian saw me off as I motored towards the Vincent Thomas Bridge that stands above the Los Angeles Harbor. The channel was a glow with golden light from the setting sun and my usual surroundings of massive cargo ships and their shore sides cranes appeared warm and cinematic.

My nerves were a wreck. This was to be my first ever single-handed passage of any notable distance, 77 nautical miles, not to mention my first major sailing trip solo to an island with no facilities and likely few, if any, other boats out there due to this being December. The Channel Islands can be dicey this time of year due to a local wind event we have in Southern California known as the "Santa Anas". The Santa Ana winds are a katabatic wind that originate in the Great Basin and find their way to the sea, increasing in speed as they are forced through the canyons of the mountain ranges. The winds are hot and dry and can be extremely dangerous both on land and even more so at sea if you find yourself with a lee shore. Two separate Santa Ana wind events the weeks prior to my trip very nearly forced me to change my entire passage and head for the backside of Catalina Island, Santa Barbara Island or possibly San Nicolas Island. I watched the weather forecasts for weeks leading up to my departure and the night before I was to leave I decided to go for it as the likelihood of another Santa Ana spell seemed slim.

The first three anchorages I planned to visit were all on the south side of the Santa Cruz Island and had been protected from the last few periods of high wind. It is said that if you see a swell coming from the east (the direction of the mainland) or feel hot air that feels like it is from a hair dryer you should leave the anchorage immediately as these are signs of the Santa Anas and soon you will have a lee shore. My feeling was that if I needed to bail out and head from Catalina I could, but I needed to have a go at my original float plan and this trip I had been dreaming about for years.

As I passed Angels Gate Light, the darkness of night had settled in. I had my mainsail up, my headsail rigged and ready and the wind apparently had the night off so the diesel engine worked steadily with its characteristic knock, knock, knock, a sound that makes a gas engine owner listen in with dread. We are motoring at about 3.5 knots / 2500 rpm and as I made my turn west out of the shipping channel I instantly find myself in a minefield of lobster pot buoys many of which are either dark blue or black and nearly impossible to see. I looked south and could not see any easy way out then looked north and saw the breakwater. I am amazed that such a practice is legal so close to a major shipping channel and active harbor. This was absolutely the LAST place I wanted to get propped, with no wind, at night, adjacent to a major port. I stood up on the cockpit seats and steered the tiller with my foot as I squinted into the darkness maneuvering in and out of the buoys. This dance went on for over an hour before I was finally free of the obstacles.

At around midnight the swell had picked up and was working in unison with my exhaustion to make me start feeling seasick. I don't get seasick often but when I am on a boat that is bobbing about from swell and no wind to dig the boat in, my eyeballs start feeling like they are not in alignment and I take this as a sign to take a Dramamine immediately. I had purchased and installed a Raymarine st2000+ Autotiller but even after calibrating it two separate times it refused to hold my course. I would set it up, set my course, hit "auto" and soon it would round up and spin us in a circle. At first I thought maybe my prop walk was too much for it, but then I tried it while simply sailing and it did the same thing. I ended up just keeping it attached to the tiller and using it as a "lashing" and simply hitting the +1 / -1 to adjust my course as needed.

Keeping an eye on my new AIS system I had also installed for this trip, I could see the direction and speed of the cargo ships in the shipping lane that was just west of me. I waited for a good window as two ships passed one another and cut across the shipping lanes and the zone of separation and got well above the lanes before readjusting my course and heading north west on a bearing of 283° pointing directly towards my first anchorage, Coches Prietos.

The night was a chilly 55 degrees and I sat in the cockpit in long johns, pants, Musto foulies, Sorel boots, a t-shirt, hoodie and Helly Hansen jacket. Which I am sure for anyone who lives outside of Southern California and has to experience REAL cold and weather this is laughable, but nonetheless we are a delicate bunch here in Los Angeles when the temperature drops below 70 degrees. Oh yes I almost forgot, I was also sitting in a sleeping bag.

With my AIS alarm on, a bed made out of cockpit cushions and a timer set, I lay down against the cabin bulkheads and napped in 10-minute increments. It would go like this: timer goes off, I sit up look around slowly in a complete circle looking for lights, check and adjust my course if needed, look at AIS, reset timer for 10 minutes and lay back down. After an hour of this I allowed myself 15 minutes then to 20 minutes. By 5 am I was rested enough to stay up and could clearly see the lighthouse on Anacapa Island signalling me with regularity as I motored towards the islands.

A few dolphins visited me in the night and then more paid a visit at 6:30 am as the sun was rising. Any sailor will tell you the best watch is the one that comes with a sunrise. The experience is hard to describe for anyone whom hasn't done an overnight passage onboard a sailboat. The stillness of the morning as the night moves west and the sun causally climbs preceded by the gradients of twilight, having this to one's self while at sea makes you feel an ownership to the experience, to the magic. It is yours and yours alone.

Once the sun was up and done with its spell upon me I had some chopped peaches and pears for breakfast, as my stomach was still shaky, though I never did throw up thanks to the Dramamine.

Soon I could see Santa Cruz Island and the higher portion of Anacapa. It's amazing how close you can seem to an island and then it still take you 4 hours to reach it. It was very clear out and during sunrise I could clearly see where "Yellow Banks Anchorage" was from the photo and description in Brian Fagan's book "Cruising Guide to Southern California's Offshore Islands". This book is truly an incredible resource and essential for anyone planning on sailing to the Channel Islands.

I decided to bite the bullet and try my first drone flight from the boat. There was almost no wind so I thought this was the best time to try it for the first time. The take off went off without a hitch and I flew up and around, my heart racing, and getting some amazing shots of the boat sailing next to Santa Cruz Island…. Well I would have if I had hit record. The landing was very nerve wracking but I got it done.

For a while I kept thinking I could see the rock face of Albert's Anchorage but what I was looking at turned out to be Blue Banks. Finally as I approached I saw two sailing vessels and a single fishing boat anchored in Albert's Anchorage and they waved as I passed by. I was happy to see no one was anchored in Coches Prietos (most likely the other vessels knew how rolly it was with this swell and dropped the hook at Albert's instead).

I got the hook set in 25' of water and let out 4:1 scope. Anchored behind a kelp bed that I had hoped would help with the swell. I should have anchored even closer ashore to be even more protected but this being my first anchorage alone I was nervous and the shore, rocks and cliffs walls all seem extremely close to someone with no experiences anchoring in such a setting.

I had a good deal of experience anchoring from my time onboard SY Selkie in the Orkney Islands of Scotland in 2014. We sailed all throughout the Orkney Isles anchoring nightly and I was always the one dropping the hook and letting out scope as the captain, Celia Bull, directed. The tides in the UK are so much greater than anything we have in California that on one occasion we anchored deep into Otters Wick bay on the island of Sanday. The captain knew the tide would pull out about a mile and planned accordingly by raising the lifting keel on the custom-built 51ft aluminium sloop. As the tide fled and the waters edge crept its way towards the North Sea, Selkie sat flat upon the sandy bottom that was marked only by small mounds of sand in someone keyhole shapes made by the Razor Clams whom where hiding beneath the surface of the sand. As the captain gave the now exposed hull a once over I went over to see the anchor set in its place now sitting in the open air. All of the anchorages we visited in the Orkney Isles were in large open bays and none had prepared me for the feeling that I was desperately close to the cliff walls, a fear that was completely unfounded I discovered only after I had recorded myself from above with my drone the next morning.

After I was sure the hook was set and all was good I tidied up the boat and got everything in order. The anchorage was very rolly so I deployed a Rocker Stopper, which is a series of plastic rings that hang one below the other with a line connecting them all. You rig it to the end of your boom and a preventer going forward then push the boom out and tighten everything down. The drag on the rings dampens the rolling of the boat in a bad swell and surely made my night's sleep much more pleasant.

As I sat on the deck taking in my surroundings of the peace anchorage, I was treated to a large bald eagle soaring over the anchorage and landing on a rock atop the cliff and looking down upon Triteia and myself.

The sunset upstaged the sunrise and soon the sky was a hot pink that cannot be captured in photography, video or the written word. Colors of such dramatic brilliance seem so unnatural and yet shows of beauty such as these have been taking place since before eyes even existed on the planet Earth.

    I made my way into the cabin and made some dinner. I had already set up my laptop at the nav station and set my anchor alarm on Open CPN, the route planning software I use on my computer. I use iNavX on my iPhone for navigation while under way but I really enjoy Open CPN for its anchor alarm and the easy for planning passages. I watched the shapes made by Triteia moving on the hook in the swells as I ate my dinner and prepared to sleep. It was Christmas Eve, the most important night of all in the minds of many children. I thought about my mother and my childhood and the wonderful anticipation this night had brought me as a small boy. I knew this Christmas morning was going to bring me something special as well. My first ever night on anchor alone and onboard my own boat.

    Completely beat from the nearly 23-hour passage I turned in at 17:30 sleeping on the port settee so I could have quick access to the deck and I could open one eye and see the laptop if need be. I slept for almost 12 hours waking only twice, once at 1 and once at 4 to check on the anchor. Each time I was greeted by a sky full of twinkling stars free from the light pollution of the city. I hope Santa smiled as he flew past.

POSITION LOG:

16:30 – 33°45'52"N 118°15'03"W
Departed

18:00 – 33°41'67"N 118°16'19"W
Underway

00:00 – 33°43'02"N 118°38'00"W
Underway

07:00 – 33°48'48"N 119°07'82"W
Underway

12:30 – 33°56'52"N 119°31'13"W
Underway

15:00 – 33°58'05"N 119°42'25"W
Anchored

- Departure -

- Passing Angels Gate Lighthouse -

- Highly Stressful Drone Flight -

- Approaching Santa Cruz Island -

- Approaching Coches Prietos -

- Coches Prietos -

- On the hook after at Coches Prietos -

- Christmas Eve Sunset at Coches Prietos -

- CHAPTER 2 -

Coches Prietos
and the passage to
Morse Point Anchorage

8 nm | 3.5 hours | Motorsail

December 25 2017
33°58'05"N 119°42'25"W

    I awoke on Christmas morning at 5:00 in the stillness of Coches Prietos Anchorage and made some coffee and oatmeal. The anchorage was dark and quiet and very peaceful and the motion of the boat at anchor was somewhat euphoric. Soon the sun was rising and the sky grew more brilliant by the minute as the day emerged and the cliffs surrounding me were hues of pink as the sky brightened with a neon pink.

    This was the very reason I had first been interested in sailing. Years ago I was camping in Big Sur in a beautiful and serene location and a number of the other campers were playing loud music and being generally obnoxious. I remember thinking "I need to learn how to sail so I can take a boat out in the middle of nowhere and wake up, walk on deck with coffee in my hand and not see another human for miles." It was a very long time between that first desire and this moment but it had finally come to fruition.

    I sat on the deck, hot cup of coffee in hand with seals lazily eating their breakfast next to the boat in the kelp beds and only the sound of the sea lapping at Triteia and rolling across the rocks. This was why I wanted to sail, peaceful mornings on the hook in beautiful places and I am happy to take all the hard work and struggles that go along with it.

    In classic human form I retrieved my drone from the cabin to get some footage of the scene (Something that would have been extremely obnoxious for any fellow yachties trying to enjoy a peaceful morning in the anchorage, thankfully I was alone and didn't disturb anyone)

    I positioned the drone on the companion way hatch with the boom swung out and took off from the flat boat that was not moving.... And BAM it hit the backstay and flipped several times before righting itself no more than 4 inches from the water. My heart exploded in my chest as I made it climb away from a watery grave. After safely getting her above the anchorage, I took video of Triteia under anchor at our first ever anchorage together. The access to such technology on a consumer level is really remarkable and allows us to see the beauty of a sailboat at sea or at anchor from a perspective not previously possible to the common sailor. I feel blessed to live in such a time to experience such settings not only from the surface of the sea but also from the perspective of the birds looking down with wonder.

    On the beach I could see signs that said "No Trespassing" so I didn't bother launching the dinghy and going ashore here. I think this section of the island is under rehabilitation and visitors are not allowed to hike or explore here as the Nature Conservancy works to restore the land and its native plants.

Just before 9 am I began stowing everything away and preparing to pull up the hook and move on to Morse Point Anchorage. I checked the oil and discovered, to my dismay, it was nearly bone dry. I changed the oil before I left and put in all new oil but I didn't think to buy extra oil. While scratching my head and staring at the engine I see a shiny nut in the bilge and reach in and retrieve it. It belonged to one of the bolts that secure my motor mounts to the steel frame the engine sits on. Two of the other nuts had also vibrated loose but had not fallen off yet. On the passage over I had motored 22.5 hours continuously and this was my far the longest I had run the Yanmar 2gm20f since installing her. Being a novice on diesel engines I can only assume that the vibrations of the engine that slowly loosened her bolts had contributed to the drastic depletion of oil. I later discovered diesel engines burn oil faster than their gasoline-drinking cousins.

Now I found myself with some serious concern with this oil situation. I remembered the few yachts that were anchored around the corner at Albert's Cove and decided to have a look and see if they were still there when I headed out and see if I could buy some oil from them if they had any to spare.

Finishing up my preparations for departure I hauled up the hook for the first time. I had gone to great trouble building out the anchor locker and installing the Lofrans manual windlass for the trip but to my dismay the "wildcat", a metal ring that receives the chain and pulls the anchor up as you crank the handle, was the wrong size for my set up. I have 80' of 3/8 BBB chain and the wildcat on my windlass seems to be for 5/8 sized chain.

So in a true right of passage I started hauling up the anchor by hand, the first of many times over the next week. Alone, inexperienced and solo anchoring and pulsing with fear and anxiety of being close to the cliffs I pulled the anchor up until it was hanging about 10 feet below the bow and I hurried back to the cockpit in what must have looked like a frantic state to the nearby seals watching and judging me. Once in the cockpit, I motored out to deeper water slowly with the anchor hanging well below my four-foot draft. Once I felt comfortable about my distance from all the dangers I imagined were laying in wait, I went forward and finished the job and got my 35lb delta style anchor secured.

I motored out and peeked around the corner at Albert's Cove and could see the sailing yachts that had been anchored there a distance down the coast heading east. I was western bound and knew I couldn't catch them and decided I would continue on my way and hopefully would come across another boat at Morse Point.

As I cleared Bowen Point and turned west I could already see Gull Island in the distance. This large boulder coming out of the sea lays between Malva Real Anchorage and Morse Point Anchorage. The distance was only 8 nm and I motored at 2000 rpm to try and not push the engine anymore than I had to. It was a pleasant and warm day, bright and clear. I raised the headsail when the wind freshened but what wind was there was on the nose so it did me no good.

I passed several nice anchorages on the way and was escorted for sometime by a few pods of lazy dolphins, and possibly porpoises, some of them had very small fins and could have just been another type of dolphin. A few larger ones came over and checked me out first then more would come by as they made their way along with me. From the look of their speed I would say it's safe to assume they were also on a vacation.

I remembered that I had a quart of Magic Mystery Oil and some Two Stroke oil onboard. I would put those in my engine as soon as I was anchored. It's obviously not ideal but at least it's some sort of lubricant.

It only took me three hours of motorsailing to reach Morse Point and the oil alarm chirped a few times as I neared my anchorage and would squawk at low rpms. It never went off fully.

I made my way past Gull Island and up into the anchorage hugging along side a string of rocks and kelp that jet out from the shore creating a natural swell break, I hope anyway. I anchored kind of far from the shore with the idea that if my motor had trouble in the morning I could wait for the winds to pick up and sail off of the hook if I was safely away from land.

Anchoring in 25 feet of water, 4:1 scope and set the hook. I then took down the main and got the dinghy in the water and the deck cleared and organized, after which I put most of the magic mystery oil in the engine and a little bit of the 2-stroke oil. I started it back up and the alarm didn't sound at low RPMs so I took that as a good sign.

The wind picked up to what felt like 7 knots or so bringing the surf on the shore up. I could hear it crashing on the rocks and on the beach making Triteia a little rolly but not enough to deal with the rocker stopper. I made myself some lunch and worked on some boat projects then in the late afternoon I saw a small boat motoring towards me. When they came closer it was apparent they were coming over to Triteia so I went on deck. They pulled along side and asked if I was going to be here all night? And I said yes and I asked if they were fishing and he said "No, No, looking for dive spot" in a thick Russian accent. It was two guys in a small boat in the middle of nowhere and the boat didn't seem to have any provisions of place to sleep or anything onboard so I assume they were with a nearby fishing boat I could see just past Gull Island.

I asked if they had any engine oil and he said they did not, he did offer me some WD40 but I thanked him and declined. I asked him if they were diving for lobsters and he said they were just diving for fun, but it didn't seem that way to me since he asked if I would be there all night. Not sure, it felt sketchy.

At sunset the sun made his way slowly into the drink. The air was the freshest I think I have ever smelled in all my 44 years on this planet. I watched as that perfect orange orb slipped into the night.

POSITION LOG:

09:00 – 33°58'05"N 119°42'25"W
Departed

13:30 – 33°57' 97"N 119°50' 65"W
Anchored
4:1 in 25'

LOG NOTES:

* Discovered Engine is out of oil
* Glassy passage to Morse Point
* Towing Dinghy Slowed Speed

- Sunrise at Coches Prietos -

- Birds eye view of SV Triteia on the hook -

- Departing Coches Prietos -

- Friends -

- Approaching Morse Point -

- On the Hook at Morse Point -

- On the Hook at Morse Point -

- Sunset at Morse Point -

- Chapter 3 -

Morse Point
and the passage to
Forney Cove Anchorage

7 nm | 3 hours | Motorsail

December 26 2017
33°57'97"N 119°50'65"W

I awoke in the night nervous about the anchor. The anchor alarm didn't sound and the winds were light but I was still green when it comes to being under anchor on my own boat. Walking on deck all appeared fine but I recall the breaking waves on the shore sounding so very close and their faint glow seemed even closer still. I stood for a long time trying to decide if I had been dragging closer to the shore and maybe the anchor alarm wasn't working properly. I went below and checked Open CPN and it showed my anchor sway drawn on the computer screen and all looked correct. I went back on deck and listened some more before going back to my berth and sleeping.

As the tides changed shifts in the night the anchorage became even rollier making for a less than ideal conditions for sleeping. I awoke at 6:30 in the morning and watched the sun start his day.

The waves crashing ashore were more than I wanted to attempt in my dinghy so I decided to not go explore on land. I had already put the dinghy in the water so I decided to just tow her behind for the sail to Forney Cove that was 8 nm to the Northwest.

Aft Note: In hindsight I feel I shortchanged myself on both Coches Prietos and Morse Point by not going ashore for a walk and a view of Triteia. With Coches Prietos it was a combination of nerves and exhaustion from the passage. My hesitation to go ashore at Morse Point was the breakers on the beach, which would have been tricky for sure but I think I would have had a different connection with this anchorage had I made my way ashore.

After getting everything ready for the sail to Forney Cove I started the engine and was pleased to hear the oil alarm didn't go off in low RPMs. Seems like the magic mystery oil and 2 stroke oil I added is helping even if just a bit.

The motorsail from Morse Point to Forney Cove was easy with no sounding of from the engine alarm. With the dinghy in tow I lost half a knot of speed, which was a bummer, but the wind freshened and the main got me to 3.8 instead of 2.9, I will not be towing the dinghy again.

The coastline was stunning with little to no current evidence of man; no power lines, no fences, no signs, no cars and only a few structures exist on the entire island today. There has long been a human presence on Santa *Cr*uz Island from the Chumash people to early Spanish sailors to modern ranchers. But the island today feels like it has been taken back to a time before all of that. It seems so unspoiled and seemingly unchanged since a time before man and all of his clutter.

As I motored along I passed by Christy Anchorage, which looked lovely but not very well protected. Its long sandy beach can be seen stretching from Kinton Point to Black Point and sits at the far end of the large bay that Forney's Cove also belongs to.

The kelp wasn't very thick this time of year making the entrance to Forney's wide open. A drawing in Fagen's book showed that you might have to navigate through dense kelp to find your way into the anchorage. The kelp appeared to get thicker as you got closer to shore so I sounded my way in as close as I could without getting in the mess of it. Settling on a spot to drop the hook in 22' of water my anchor found her way to the sandy bottom and set. I let out 4 to 1 scope as the anchorage felt very protected by the large rocks and reefs that frame out Forney's Cove. It was 11:45 am and I was already secured in my new anchorage.

With the dinghy already in the water I wasted no time getting ashore to explore. Clamping my gopro camera on the front of the dinghy to document my first solo shore landing. As I tried to get situated in the dinghy I lost my balance and nearly capsized reaching to brace myself on the boat, dunking myself half underwater up to my left shoulder. My little sabot righted herself and kept me from going all the way in. I was glad to have captured it on camera so all of my friends could get a good laugh out of it. Regaining my composure I paddled ashore and found a nice sandy spot to shoot for. The break was very mellow and as I paddled furiously at the calm break, being both nervous and cautious at my first landing, I surfed a small wave in and slid nicely up on the beach, which was great fun.

Pulling the dinghy high up on the dry sand I tied the painter line off to a large stone to ensure she would be there when I returned regardless of the tides. The sand was covered with countless fox tracks from the islands unique little "Island Fox", a species that only exists on the Channel Islands.

I made my way over to check out the tide pools and came across a massive rusty engine block and other steel pieces from an old shipwreck that had met its fate on the rocks. There was a limited variety of life in the tide pools mostly just the common anemones, snails and limpets. I climbed up the sandy hill and made my way over towards Fraser Cove. The landscape was that of tall grasses, succulents and even some cactus. I also saw a few sweet wild flowers still blooming even in December.

Standing above Fraser Cove I was amazed at how Jurassic this side of the island looks; barren, rough and fantastic. Hiking down to Fraser beach the rocks looked like a place a dragon could be seen lounging in any given fantasy movie, red, cracked and fragmented rocks everywhere, very unusual.

Making my way up towards the highest point I could see a hill that had a large "void" between it and Fraser Point. It looked like man had excavated it until I got above and peered over the edge and could clearly see the waves had dug the cliff side out to nothing, but in a very square and structured way.

The sea churned violently below me around the rocks making the water a beautiful light blue in color. Swirling eddies revealed rocks hidden beneath the water's surface making any sailor shutter at the thought of the unseen. Seeing the seas unsettled even on this calmest of days made me wonder what this shore would look like in rough weather with the wind roaring past Point Conception which is only 34 nm from Fraser Point and the seas standing up to double headers. This is certainty not a shore you want in your lee.

I continued my hike making my way up to the top of Fraser Point's highest cliff. Checking my cell phone I saw I finally had service so I sent off a few messages to friends and family. I messaged my brother Colby about my oil situation and explained I thought everything would be fine but I wanted someone to know what was going on.

I sat for a while watching the sea and a few large ravens came over to check me out. They got very close and surveyed the scene to see if I had any food for them. I made my way back down to the shore and hurried back out to the boat to get my drone and camera so I could get some footage of the sunset that was fast approaching.

My dinghy is an old sailing sabot made of fiberglass. I bought her for $40 years before I had Triteia in an effort to feel like I was making progress on my dream even while I wanted to find my real boat. I patched up all of her holes and repaired her gunwales. I really like having a hard dinghy for a variety of reasons; you can stand up inside them and still have relatively stable footing, you can load them up with all manner of gear, provisions or water jugs and they maintain their shape, and they row much better than inflatable dinghies. Their cons are that they are difficult to store on deck compared to a dinghy you can deflate and roll up and they are MUCH heavier to get in and out of the water with. When a single sailor is in them paddling or rowing they sure make quick business of the trip though. I made my way over the kelp forests between the Triteia and the shore, peering in the water as I passed I could see their stalks reaching up towards the surface looking like a hundred massive vines hanging up instead of down.

I quickly grabbed my camera gear from the boat, CAREFULLY got back in the dinghy (I also placed all the electronics in a waterproof bag) and made my way back to the shore.

Once back on the beach I set up my Canon camera and started a time-lapse then I took to the sky with my drone and documented this incredible setting from a birds eye view. The golden light of magic hour was making this already stunning landscape glow in a manner that felt more cinematic that real.

I was amazed at the power in my hands to see this landscape from such a perspective. Only in very recent history could the average person have access to record his or her memories in a way that previously was only possible if you had access to a plane or helicopter and a big budget. I made my way up above the boat and looked down upon it. I could clearly see the kelp beds in the anchorage. Pointing the drone towards the land it felt like I was watching an epic movie based in prehistory. These are the sights I longed to see, to be the only person around, surrounded by beauty. This is what the months of long days were for preparing the boat, the bloody knuckles, the stress, the 16-hour days. It was all for these types of experiences.

As the sun steadily showed himself out I gathered up my things, loaded them back into the dinghy, drug her back to the water and slowly paddled back to the boat, taking it all in. How on earth did I find myself in such a truly beautiful place such as this? All to myself with only the sounds of the sea and stillness that is absent from most of our daily lives. The air seemed impossibly crisp as the stars arrived for their night shift, unspoiled by the city lights.

Back onboard Triteia I made myself some dinner and turned in for the night. The entire trip so far I had been sleeping on the port settee but on this night I decided to be luxurious and sleep forward in the V-Berth. As I climb into my sea-nest and settle in I hear a very annoying CLANK, CLANK, CLANKING sound. If you have ever spent the night on a boat under anchor you know that the first 20 minutes of attempting to sleep are spent locating sounds and finding ways to stop the sounds from happening. Shoving t-shirts between doors, rearranging galley cupboards to stop cups or cans from rolling, getting scientific to figure out how to stop a mystery squeak that seems to come from nowhere. This particular sound, the "clank, clank, clank" I identified immediately without even lifting my head and that is because I instantly knew that my own foolish decision had created this nuisance.

A little back story about this subject, Triteia was originally equipped with half rope / half wire cable running rigging. The main halyard, jib halyard and spinnaker halyard were all wire cable from the canvas to the block then just past the block down was rope. One of the first things I had done when I got the boat was replace the main halyard, jib halyard, topping lift and mainsheet. I couldn't afford to replace the spin halyard at that time and since I don't have a spinnaker anyway I decided to wait and just leave the original for now as a way to hoist tool buckets up top when I was aloft working.

Earlier in the trip the wire cable part of the Spinnaker halyard kept tapping on the mast every so slightly at night which was making me a little crazy. So as I was preparing to depart from Morse Point I had a brilliant idea: Cut down the Spin Halyard!!! Problem solved!

What I didn't realize was that in doing so I was leaving the block aloft swinging freely which was now producing the much more annoying "clank, clank, clank" sound I was hearing as I lay in my seemingly palatial V-berth. All sounds produced by something coming in contact with the mast, whether it is loose wires running inside the mast or in this case an errant block, are amplified by the deck and cabin making them much louder inside than out. Think of it like putting your ear to a drinking glass and the glass to a door to hear what is on the other side. I had experienced this before with a 26' Excalibur I shared with a friend a few years back. The electrical wires in the mast on that boat made such a racket that it made sleeping on the boat very difficult.

Luckily for me the sound of the block was muted in the main cabin so I returned to my rightful place on the port settee like a scolded dog that tried to sneak into the big bed only to be sent back to his regular sleeping spot. My nerves where finally calming down as I now trusted the boat and had a clearer vision of her, and my, limitations and slowly gained more confidence in my ability towards problems as they arise (aside from the wire halyard decision that is).

POSITION LOG:

09:00 – 33°57'97"N 119°50'65"W
Departed

12:00 – 34°03' 36"N 119°55'14"W
Anchored
4:1 in 22'

LOG NOTES:

*Put 5 gallons of diesel in the tank
*Scattered kelp beds (at Forney cove)
*Oil seems OK

*Went Ashore – 13:20 – 15:20
*Went Ashore – 16:00 – 17:30

- A Glassy Passage -

- Graceful Entry -

- Bay and Forney Cove -

- Forney Cove -

- Forney Cove -

- Forney Cove -

- Forney Cove -

- What all the hard work is for -

- Chapter 4 -

Forney Cove
and the passage to
Cueva Valdez Anchorage

8 nm | 4 hours | Sail

December 27, 2017
34°03'36"N 119°55'14"W

I had a restful night's sleep in the lovely protected anchorage of Forney's Cove. As I prepared to weigh anchor and head out to my next anchorage I decided I would try and go up to the top of the mast and take down the loose block.

     I made a homemade mast climber rope ladder when I got Triteia so I could work up top alone. It is a simple design, just a very long rope with foot loops tied in it that you hoist with a halyard and tie off the other end to the deck and tighten it as best you can for stability, well the word stability should not be used when speaking about this mast climber I can assure you of that. While it is not ideal it does give me some option when I need to go up and have no one there to help me. I usually climb to the spreaders then clip a line around my waist and around the mast so that if I fall from further up I will only fall to the spreaders. For the record this thing is sketchy even when tied up at the dock at the marina.

     Setting up my GoPro to film my attempt; success or failure or worse. The motion of the boat under anchor combined with my added weight up top exaggerated the swaying of the mast greatly. I made it up to the spreaders then half way up from the spreaders to the masthead before I gave up and came back down. It will just have to wait until I return to the marina to take it down.

     I finished getting the boat ready for departure and made my way out of the calm anchorage of Forney Cove, by far my favorite anchorage of the trip.

     The original plan was to sail to Lady's Harbor anchorage but to anchor there you need to tuck in and drop a stern anchor and a bow anchor and I am not comfortable doing this solo yet so I decided on Cueva Valdez anchorage instead. I hauled up the hook at 10:30 am giving myself plenty of time for the day's passage that was only 7 nautical miles out and around.

     Just past the rocks it became very clear how protected the anchorage really was as the swells were well over 3 feet closer to 4 feet. Once I got out past all the lobster pots I was able to kill the engine and sail close hauled with a fresh morning breeze that was making its way through the Santa Cruz Channel that runs between Santa Rosa Island and Santa Cruz Island. Fraser Point was soon off of our starboard bow. The point looked incredible with the trace of fog lingering from the night.

     Sailing at about 5 knots until we rounded the point and the winds died off outside of the channel, I pointed out to sea to take advantage of what wind there was and to give myself more sea room. After about half an hour of flogging I finally got the sails to set wing and wing and made my way down the north side of the island.

I sailed past the famous "Painted Cave" but the light silhouetted the shore and hid it from view. I wouldn't have even noticed it had it not been for a fishing boat that stopped to check it out. Santa Cruz's "Painted Cave" is the longest sea cave in North America and one of the lengthiest in the world. Tall enough to drive a 60-foot boat into, the cave goes into the side of the island a quarter of a mile. Being that I am alone and in a full-keeled sailing yacht I was unable and unwilling to go in for a closer look. A motor yacht can easily maneuver close in and have a look but backing up an Alberg 30 under motor is only doable if you have a large open area and enjoy backing up in circles. So I would have to wait for another trip to explore the Painted Cave.

Aft Thought: I returned to Santa Cruz Island a few months after this on a dive boat with my little brother and the Captain of that boat took us inside the cave and it was remarkable!

It felt as if I was making almost no headway and I check Navionics to see how fast we were going to my surprise it showed we were sailing at about 3.5 knots! This was the same speed we would have been doing under motor, as I didn't want to push my oil-starved engine anymore than I had to. I relaxed knowing that we were making good headway with plenty of time before sunset and a warm sun shining down through clear skies.

Soon we were sailing past Hazards Anchorage and its sandy beach, this was a good marker visually for following along on the paper chart and keeping track of where we were the old fashioned way. Before I knew it, Cueva Valdez was on my starboard beam so I dropped the sails and turned on the motor. As I crept into this new anchorage I could see spouts from baby dolphins glowing in the sunlight close to shore then their mother surfaced near me to check out the boat and determine our intentions. She was covered in what looked like white scars and had an unusual dorsal fin and shape. They turned out to be Risso Dolphins, the first and only I have ever seen.

I dropped the hook in 25 feet of water, set it and killed the engine. Looking around at my new setting I was amazed at how cool this anchorage was. Sea caves surrounded me and there was a nice sandy beach that would make for an easy landing for exploration.

Racing the daylight I launched my dinghy and went to check out the sea caves by water and on land. The swell was mellow allowing me to paddle up to the eastern most caves for a look before making my way ashore to see the western most caves. Pulling my dinghy high and dry I walked across the beach to the large cave. The sound of the sea rolling across the rocks echoing and amplified by the cave was very soothing. Once inside the cave I was given a fantasy-esque view of Triteia through the mouth of a cave. I continued my hike out the other side and came across a cool sea stack that some birds were lounging on. Climbing out as far as possible on foot I could see caves scattered all along the cliffs base making for an extensive network of hiding spots for seals and other sea creatures.

Climbing over the rocks I made my way back to the dinghy as the sun ducked behind the island and a long shadow made its way across the bay. Back onboard the boat I was treated to a beautiful sunset with pink clouds hanging over and in front of the mainland. A small lobster boat motored into the anchorage as the darkness set it.

The night was very rolly. In my hand written journal it reads "The night was very, very, very rolly". So rolly in fact I had to move my bedding to the cabin sole so that I could pin myself between the port and starboard settees. Once in the secure position I fell right to sleep.

At 12:30 am my anchor alarm went off pulling me instantly out of the deepest of sleeps. I got up and looked at Open CPN, the software I use on my laptop for route planning and my anchor watch. This software records the spider-web like motion of the boat under anchor and on the screen I could clearly see that there was a little "bump" outside of what had been the regular chaos field of recorded movements. I went on deck and looked at the anchor rode and it wasn't pulled taught and all looked normal. There was also no wind to speak of and the worst part of the swell had subsided. Going back down below I wondered if I had just maybe entered too tight of a margin in the anchor alarm settings as for some reason it would only let me enter the desired distance and scope in meters so it was possible I had just done the math wrong maybe. I reset the alarm; not adjusting any settings just simply reset it and lay back down.

Ten minutes later the alarm went off again so I got up and went on deck and let out another 40' of rode. I then went to the cockpit to start the engine to reset the anchor and the engine did not want to start. It would start and then die and sounded as tired as I felt. This was a very scary moment for me considering my anchor was dragging. I finally got it started and reset the anchor making sure it was well dug in as the rope was completely taught and we were not moving backwards at all. Resetting the anchor alarm as well, I returned to my cozy cabin floor to try and get some sleep with my nerves completely frayed. The rest of the night the alarm did not sound and we held fast.

> *Aft Thought: I think about how stressful this was for me, being new to single handed cruising, and then I think about how this happened in perfect weather with plenty of distance between me and the shore. I can't imagine how stressful this situation would have been in a blow with a lee shore. Sometimes a scenario can seem very dire because we lack real world experience in dealing with something like an anchoring dragging in the middle of the night. I was lucky enough to have had this experience in a very calm controlled setting with plenty of room between the boat and the beach/cliffs. I am certain that in the future I will be awoken at night in terrible conditions with a dragging anchor in a far flung anchorage a world away from Santa Cruz Island but when I do I will have a confidence gained from this very night that will help me know that the problem can be conquered.*
>
> *Moral of the story: Always try and lay out 7 scope ladies and gentlemen. The best way to deal with an anchor dragging is to do everything you can before hand to prevent it from dragging.*

POSITION LOG:

10:30 – 34° 03'36"N 119°55'14"W
Departed

14:30 – 34°03'22"N 119°49'07"W
Anchored
4:1 in 25'

LOG NOTES:

*Sailed the entire way!!!
*Good speed with light wind and swell behind me
*Very warm on this side of the island
*Went Ashore – 15:20 – 16:00

- Sketchy Mast Climb Under Anchor -

- Sailing Around the Western Point -

- Sailing -

- Greetings from a Rizzo Dolphin -

- Triteia on the Hook at Cueva Valdez -

- The Sea Caves of Cueva Valdez -

- SV Triteia -

- Day is Done -

- Chapter 5 -

Cueva Valdez
and the passage to
Pelican Bay Anchorage

7 nm | 2 hours | Motorsail

December 28, 2017
34° 03' 22"N 119° 49' 07"W

    I awoke at sunrise feeling I hadn't slept at all. Between the rolliness of the anchorage and the anchor dragging incident I was completely exhausted so much so that I poured my instant coffee packet in my oatmeal bowl. After some breakfast and much needed coffee I went up on deck and noticed the lobster boat was named "Miss Mae" and that they were on deck getting ready to start their day. My grandma's name was Eva Mae so I took this as a sign and got my dinghy back in the water as quickly as I could.

    The muted sunrise slowly grew brighter as I rowed over to small fishing boat. With my approached the deckhand Jerome greeted me with "Another day in paradise!"

    I ask them if I could buy some oil from them because I was in a bad way and the Captain, Chris, immediately went below. Jerome told me I had a beautiful Triton (Tritons were also designed by Carl Alberg so that was a pretty good guess). Captain Chris reemerged with a 5-gallon container that he had filled more than half full of oil for me. They wouldn't accept any money and we talked a bit about their trade. I thanked them profusely and rowed back to my boat sooooo relieved! My attitude towards lobster pots has changed forever.

    Once back on Triteia I topped off my oil and ran the engine for a while. She sounded much better and I felt so relieved. The stress of not having oil had weighed me down so much that it was always on my mind and now that massive weight had been lifted and I felt so relaxed. With my newly gained sense of comfort I rowed back ashore and explored the shore and caves as the sun worked his way up to start his day.

    Back at the boat with the dinghy stored in its rightful place on the foredeck I grabbed the anchor chain and started my morning ritual of hauling up the 35lb anchor and 80ft of chain by hand. Each day once the anchor was on deck and secured, breathing heavily, I thought of the importance of a windlass and fantasized about what life would be like once I got the correct sized wildcat for mine.

    At 10:45 I departed Cueva Valdez with no wind to speak of. I hanked on my drifter and hoped at for another slow passage of wing and wing sailing to Pelican Bay. Pelican is only 7nm east of Cueva Valdez so the passage should only be a few hours.

    Once I got out of the anchorage I could see a massive fog bank on the horizon that I hoped was burning off and not coming in. Very quickly I could see that it was indeed coming my way and very quickly.

I dropped the headsail and pulled the main in amidships, checked my compass course and prepared to sail blind through pea soup fog.

In 2014 onboard SY Selkie I stood at the helm for four hours sailing through the thickest fog I have ever encountered in my life on land or sea. We were sailing down the west coast of Scotland's Orkney Islands "Mainland". We had departed the island of Westray and made our way south. The Captain, who taught me so much about sailing, Celia Bull, assigned 3 crew members on the bow to watch for crab pots and to call them out to me. She explained to me that with no visual of land I was to sail our intended compass course and to not look up unless I was changing course to avoid a crab pot. "They are your eyes, you drive us by the compass". The captain stayed below at the navigation station watching the radar screen to keep an eye on our distance from the cliffs and to watch out for the large ferries that ply these waters. At one point in the passage the captain came on deck and took the helm and came hard about. She said there was a large ferry very close by and she blasted our small horn. The fog was so thick that we could see no trace of the massive vessel. It got close enough to us that we could feel the sound of its engines in our chests but we never even saw a silhouette in the dense fog. We held our plotted course after avoiding the people mover and eventually the centuries old, picturesque town of Stromness emerged from the fog like a scene from a movie. We dropped the hook in the anchorage the Vikings called "Hamnavoe" which means "Safe Harbor" in English.

That experience gave me great confidence in knowing how to sail in fog: Have a plotted course and sail by compass, and radar if you have it, until you reach your safe harbor.

The fog bank closed in on me and held my course of 90°. In the thick of it the visibility was ¼ mile at sea level obscuring the island off my starboard side but it never shut the sun out and I could see blue skies above me most of the time. I was treated to the sight of a brilliant Fogbow, which is an arc of light that is the same shape as a rainbow but glows white light that is beautiful and eerie.

The fog passed within an hour. I pushed on to Pelican Bay feeling fortunate that I wasn't going to have to anchor in thick fog at an anchorage I had never visited before but soon saw another fog bank on the horizon aft so I increased my speed and wasted no time getting into the anchorage.

Laying off to drop the sails I made my way into the anchorage. Pelican Bay is a horseshoe shaped anchorage that affords great protection from the wind. It is framed with large cliff faces but appears to have no landing in the anchorage itself. As I was making my approach I noticed a small rock beach just east of the anchorage. Nervous about the cliffs, I motored around several times to find a location that I was comfortable with. There were no other boats in the anchorage so I was able to drop the hook in the middle of the bay and lay on a single hook. The guidebooks state that this is one of the most popular anchorages on Santa Cruz Island and that yachts will stack up near to the west wall to take advantage of the protection from the regular winds. When this anchorage is crowded you certainly have to have a stern anchor out as well to keep in line with all the other yachts.

I dropped the hook in 27' of water and put out 3:1 scope as I was worried about the cliffs. It felt as if I was only two boat lengths away from the large sheer cliffs, which was just an optical illusion as later in the day I would hike up above the bay and see how comically far away I actually was from the cliffs.

To take advantage of the warm weather and the solitude I decided it would be a good idea to for a skinny dip. I jumped in and almost killed myself trying to get back out of the water that was probably 55° F. Once I was back onboard Triteia I shampooed my hair, soaped up and dove back in to rinse. It was refreshing and less shocking the second time but I did not linger, as I myself am not a masochist.

I got my sabot deployed and rowed my way out of the protected bay and around the eastern end to go ashore. Once I was around the eastern most point of the anchorage I could see a beautiful valley dense with trees making their way up the mountainside. The rocky beach was at the end of a creek or wash that carried rainwater down from the hills and into the sea.

The landing was easy as the beach was well protected from the swell and soon I had my dinghy pulled high up onshore. Following a well-marked trail I made my way up to get a bird's-eye view of the anchorage. On my way I saw the Island Scrub Jay, whom only exists on this Santa Cruz Island. I also saw a number of Acorn Woodpeckers that are common in Southern California.

Continuing up the hillside I come out on top of the cliff with a wonderful view of Triteia at rest on the hook. I was truly amazed at how FAR Triteia was from the cliff side since when I was onboard it felt as if I could easily slam into it if she swung around. The perception of the distance was so confusing to me.

Remnants of the Pelican Bay Resort are still present at this lookout point. Ira Eaton and his wife Margaret lived on Santa Cruz Island full time beginning in 1910 and lived there for 27 years. Eaton captained a number of sailing vessels for fishing and chartering throughout the years and was a known character during prohibition as he stored bootleg alcohol on the adjacent Anacapa and was arrested for running a "Moonshiners School" on San Nicolas Island.

The resort at Pelican Bay grew to host more than 80 people traveling to the island to hunt, fish and swim. During the silent movie era Pelican Bay Resort regularly housed crews filming countless movies on the island. All that remains now are a few foundations of buildings, metal posts and a washed out landing at the base of the cliff.

Hiking back down and out to the beach I found a cool cave that I explored before returning to the beach when much to my joy I finally saw a rare Island Fox checking out my sabot!!! They only exist here at the Channel Islands and were almost extinct! She was smaller than a cat and so cute, I got a little bit of video of her scaling the cliff side as she went about her day.

Back on the boat I made dinner and enjoyed a beautiful sunset that was a very pronounced gradient of soft pastel colors starting with light blue to darker blue to purple to light pink to orange. It reminded me of sherbet ice cream.

After dark when I went out on deck to haul up the dinghy to keep it from banging into the hull all night as it likes to do I could hear the bay writhing with a massive school of fish. A small motor vessel had arrived at sunset and dropped anchor and the couple were sitting on their deck with a deck light on and from its reflection I could see the water alive with activity. I sat on deck for a long time enjoying the peace and listening to the waves crash into the cliffs walls slowly chiseling away sea caves with every hit.

POSITION LOG:

10:45 – 34°03'22"N 119°49'07"W
        Departed

13:00 – 34°01'99" N 119°42'14"W
        Anchored
        3:1 in 27'

LOG NOTES:

*Thick Fog Passed Through on Passage
*Motorsailed
*70° in Cabin (55° at 6am)

- Returning from Miss Mae -

- The Approaching Fog -

- Fogbow -

- Triteia on the Hook at Pelican Bay -

- The Landing at Tinkers Harbor -

- Triteia on the Hook at Pelican Bay -

- Anacapa Island in the Distance -

- Sunset at Pelican Bay -

- Chapter 6 -

Pelican Bay
and the passage to
Little Scorpion Anchorage

8.6 nm | 2.75 hours | Motorsail

December 29, 2017
34° 02' 00"N 119° 42' 14"W

I was up before the sun after an incredibly peaceful night under anchor in the most comfortable anchorage of the trip so far. Pelican Bay was so protected from the swell that it felt more like being on a lake than on an island in the Pacific Ocean. The rock cliff faces that makes up Pelican Bay made the anchorage glow in a warm light from the morning sun. Dolphins swam slowly outside the bay and a Humpback Whale steadily made his way in the direction of Chinese Harbor, which is to the east of Pelican Bay.

It's the mornings at anchor in peaceful anchorages that make all of the hard work I have done on the boat worth it. It's the very reason I was interested in learning to sail, the desire to travel by sail to out of the way places, in search of solitude, beauty, wildlife and peace.

That very moment, that was the reason.

Soon I was motoring out of the bay and heading towards the eastern most end of the island. My intended anchorage for the night was Scorpion Anchorage just around Cavern Point, a passage of just over 8 nautical miles.

There was no wind whatsoever so I motorsailed on a glassy sea. My batteries needed charging so I didn't mind the motor.

As I passed Chinese Harbor I could see a very strange haze/smoke that seemed to hover over the beach, not sure if it was from the recent fires in Ventura and Santa Barbara or what had caused it, but it was a very strange sight and had such a perfect line along its top side.

A few miles further south I can see Potato Harbor. Looking at it on the chart I could see it was a small little alcove anchorage that surely provides a beautiful spot to spend the night. From what I have read about this anchorage it is not advised in westerlies or northerlies as you will be on a lee shore and the shallow depths of the anchorage make the swell stand up if the winds increase making escape even more difficult. Would be a great place to ride out some Santa Ana's it seems.

Approaching Cavern Point I encountered a contrary current, possibly the result of an eddy created by the point, it slowed my speed at over a knot. I crept around the point to see my intended anchorage of Scorpion was littered with kayaks and an Island Packer ferry off-loading more visitors and yet another ferry on the horizon. I didn't even bother approaching the anchorage because even from this distance I could count about 20 kayaks in the water. Back to reality I suppose.

    Not being one for crowds I decided this was not the anchorage for me and motored past the large rocks that separate Scorpion from Little Scorpion to see if I wanted to drop the hook there or continue on to Smugglers Cove for the night. There was at least one large sailing vessel in Little Scorpion that I could see through the rocks as I approached and as I got the anchorage on my beam I was happy to see it was the only boat anchored there at the moment.

    I motored around the anchorage making soundings trying to find a good spot. Brian Fagen's book says to anchor as close to the large rocks as your draft will allow. The sailboat that was already there was in the sweet spot and I did not want to anchor on top of them even though my draft would have allowed me to be between them and the rocks, so I made my way further into the anchorage.

    It was a rather deep anchorage with most depths at 40ft or more but I finally found 27ft or so near to the cliffs and dropped the anchor and let out 3:1 scope, weary of having to much scope out with the cliffs nearby. After making sure the hook was set, I hung out for a bit watching the anchor alarm and trying to memorize features about my surroundings so I could have a point of reference if the anchor did drag. I felt very near to the cliffs, but after feeling the same way at Pelican Bay then seeing how far I actually was, I felt comfortable enough with the spot and decided to stay put.

    The water was so clear directly under the boat I could easily see the bottom with its mix of rocks and sand. With the sun still overhead I decided to get in the water and do some snorkeling before the sun made its way behind the island.

    Since it was December AND California waters I decided to wear my 7mm scuba wetsuit instead of the thinner 5mm wetsuit. I suited up, got my gear together and dove in. The water was so cold on my face I felt my face would shatter. Before long I had acclimated and it was tolerable, I was very glad I had decided to wear my thick scuba suit.

    Even with the remarkable visibility at depth, as you got closer in near the rocks the visibility was limited due to a strong surge that was running and the sandy bottom. I snorkeled along the cliffs and up into a sea cave. It must have been gone far back into the island as I could hear the water crashing inside far from the mouth of the cave. Being alone I only went in a very short distance before making my way back out and continued along the rocks and cliffs. It soon became obvious that it was impossible to land a dinghy in Little Scorpion and to go ashore you would need to make your way over to Scorpion either around the large rock formations or between them, though I don't know that the depths are like in the passage-ways between the two anchorages.

I continued swimming out towards the aforementioned rocks. The sunlight illuminated the sandy bottom in something of a lattice pattern that swayed and moved and was very mesmerizing. There was no kelp to speak of and very little in the way of sea life other than the ever destructive purple sea urchins.

Out at the rocks there was some sea grass and I saw my first Spanish shawl, a nudibranch (which isn't a regional nudist organization, even though it sounds like it might be) looks like a brilliantly colored, super fancy slug. Their bodies are a beautiful purple color and their backs are covered in a bright orange frills and soft spikes. Their colors are so bright they appear as if they are under a black light. I also saw a number of starfish, including a massive one that was over 12 inches across!

Making my way back to the boat after a 45-minute snorkel, I climbed back onboard and sat relaxing on the deck. The owners of the large sailboat had returned on kayaks and proceeded to haul up their anchor (with a manual windlass, which gave me great jealousy)

As they made their way off I noticed a very slight breeze on my check coming from the north through the rocks. This worried me considering where I was anchored and I check the wind forecast that still predicted it would only be 2 knots or so. I had a gut feeling that I needed to move as currently I was directly inline with an opening between one of the large rocks and the cliff side and I was worried that if the winds did pick up that channel would act as a wind funnel and make life very miserable or even dangerous for me.

I quickly pulled in the Rocker Stopper and hauled up my anchor for the 2nd time today and moved over to the sweet spot behind the largest rock while there was still daylight. After already hauling up once this morning, then going on a 45 minute swim in a strong surge my arms felt like jello and it took me a while to get the anchor hauled up a 2nd time in one day. I got it up and motored my way over close to and behind the largest of the rocks. My draft is only 4.29 inches, which allows me to get closer in than a lot of other boats. I dropped the hook again, got her set and turned on the anchor alarm.

After everything settled I made dinner and relaxed after an eventful day.

At about 5:30 pm the winds started to pick up to what felt like 10 knots and continued to increase. At 6:00 pm my anchor alarm went off. I went on deck and looked at my rode and it was very taught so I let it out to 120', reset the hook and reset the anchor alarm.

The wind report on Predict Wind still said winds were at 2 knots but when I checked the real time wind speeds on the Sailflow App for Anacapa Island it said the winds were at 10 knots with gusts of 14 which seemed about right but I would imagine it was a bit more at Little Scorpion due to the wind coming over and through the rocks. The anchor held great the rest of the night and the alarm never sounded again.

I could clearly see Anacapa Island from my new vantage point; it looked like it belonged on another planet with its strange profile

Just after sunset a motor vessel made its way in and dropped their hook further south of me. Had I not acted early in changing locations they would have surely taken the sweet spot behind the large rock. I was very glad I trusted my gut on moving before sunset and before the winds picked up and the darkness had set in. I don't think I could have hauled up the anchor by hand, alone in winds of 10 to 14 knots and I was so close to the cliffs already that letting out more scope would have proved dangerous and if my anchor had dragged at the first spot I anchored, which I am sure it would have with the wind, I would have been on a lee shore. I don't even want to think about such things. This was also a lesson to me to really look at all of your surroundings when choosing your spot. Now I will never anchor in a place where I can clearly see the geographic features could work against me. It would be better to anchor in deeper water, put out 7+ scope and deal with the swell than to pin yourself into a corner thinking that you are getting into a "protected spot". At least further out you will have the option of escape if things get dicey.

POSITION LOG:

9:30 – 34°02' 00" N 119°42' 14" W
Departed

12:15 – 34°02' 71" N 119°32' 75" W
Anchored
3:1 in 30'

15:30 – 34°02' 81" N 119°32' 76" W
hauled up / moved anchor 3:1 in 30'

18:40 – Anchor Alarm sounded
Let out rode to 120' (4:1)

LOG NOTES:

* Motorsail
* Glassy seas / no wind
* Strange smoke over Chinese Harbor
* Contrary current at 34°03' 62" N 119°34' 80" W

- A Haze Over Chinese Harbor -

- A Very Happy Sailor -

- A Stern View at Sunset -

- A Dramatic Anacapa -

- Triteia on the Hook at Little Scorpion -

- Little Scorpion Anchorage -

- Little Scorpion Anchorage -

- Little Scorpion Anchorage -

- Chapter 7 -

Little Scorpion
and the passage to
Isthmus Cove, Catalina Island

64 nm | 18.5 hours | Sail / Motorsail

December 30, 2017
34° 02'80"N 119° 32'76"W

    I awoke with the sun as usual and after making some much needed coffee I launched my drone to get some footage of the stunning setting that I was surrounded by. The fog lingered over the hills and the sunrise blanketed everything with a warm light that was beautiful and surreal. Seeing the anchorage from the sky was breathtaking and reminded me how magical this life of sailing is. That this place, so quiet, so peaceful, with unspeakable beauty is only a days sail from my home port and is mere miles from one of the largest cities in the world. How can this be? How is it that everyone on the coast isn't spending their free time on boats on our islands? I am grateful they aren't as I prefer the solitude, but it is hard to comprehend how so many boats are just sitting in the marinas.

    Taking the morning slow I did my "chores" of transferring all of my video footage, recording my "A STERN VIEW" podcast for this anchorage, doing the dishes, topping off my fuel and checking the oil and preparing to depart in the early afternoon. I saw what I believed to be a grey whale just outside the anchorage trailed by an Island Packers boat. I had seen far fewer whales on this trip than I expected I would see.

    I hauled up the anchor for the last time on Santa Cruz Island at 1 pm and motored around Little Scorpion in an attempt to recalibrate my Raymarine St2000+ Auto Tiller. It continued to not hold a course and force out hard to starboard after only a short time regardless of if we were under sail or motor so the weather helm/prop walk doesn't seem to be what is causing it to lose course. I will use it as an "electronic lashing" for the time being.

    Once I motored out of the anchorage I was able to sail right away so I pulled the kill lever on the engine. Nothing and I mean NOTHING makes me happier than turning off the engine and gracefully moving through the water under sail and silence. The magic starts when the iron genny is silenced.

    The fog had been hanging around all day long but had never come into the anchorage. Now that I was under way I could see a large fog bank, which I had hoped was simply the morning's marine layer looming in the east just past San Pedro Point. Soon it completely shrouded Anacapa Island. I had intended on sailing down the north side of Anacapa to get a look at her lighthouse and see that side of the island but with the fog I decided to just turn south through the Anacapa Passage and make my way towards Two Harbors on a course of 124°.

Anacapa is a small weathered volcanic island and the closest to the mainland in the Channel Islands chain. The name, Anacapa, is derived from the words Ennepah or Anyapakh, which means "Mirage Island" in the native Chumash language. British Naval officer George Vancouver listed it as Enecapa on his 1790 chart but the current spelling of Anacapa has been in place since 1854. It is a very strange and prehistoric looking island that is made up of three parts that meet the water. There are not any safe overnight anchorages on Anacapa but yachties can anchor in Frenchys Cove for the day and explore the island by foot, dinghy or scuba. I hope to spend some time exploring this strange desolate island in the future.

I sailed through the fog at about 2 to 3 knots and saw or heard several small fishing boats but everyone was being safe and keeping their speed down. I do not have radar on the boat so aside from my AIS I was basically sailing blind and just keeping my distance from the shipping channels. This fog was much thicker than the fog I sailed through to Pelican Bay.

At around 4 pm the sun made an appearance for a brief time illuminating Triteia in the most beautiful magic hour light and making Anacapa glow as she crept out of the fog looking like Kong Island. As I sailed in silence, surrounded by beauty my heart felt as if it would explode. This is everything I want from life. This moment and all the moments like this to come.

As night set in, the fog returned. My wind put itself to bed and I started the engine and sat down with the Raymarine Autotiller manual determined to get it working. After pouring over the book I found a section that explained how to switch the Autotiller from being configured for Port side to Starboard side. Currently it was set up for being mounted on the Port side, which is where it is installed on the boat and it shows the correct degree heading in relation to the compass. I decided to try and switch the settings to Starboard side just to see if it made a difference, now the settings show the exact opposite degree heading on the display. To my confusion and delight it worked! It held course and worked perfectly and the only problem was that the display reading is wrong and that when you make adjustments to port/starboard they are the opposite as well, but this is a very small inconvenience and having the Autotiller made my sail a thousand times easier! At this point I decided to name my Autotiller "HAL 2000".

From 10pm – 4am I slept in 20-minute naps on the deck (with my AIS alarm set) this being common practice amongst single-handed sailors and I was comfortable with this schedule after having done the same on the passage over.

Several times during the night when I would scan the horizon for ships I would hear dolphins playing at the bow. They continued to show up throughout the night and into the morning. I got up for good at 4:30am and made breakfast and was grateful how easy this passage was compared to the push north thanks to the working auto tiller. I could see Catalina's west end light by now and soon I could see Shiprock's light in the distance, which marks the entrance to the isthmus.

The final sunrise of 2017 did not disappoint. An incredible show of brilliant pink made its entrance and slowly faded into the morning. On my port beam was a very stoic looking Shiprock standing guard as the mountains of Catalina's west end stood off my starboard side. I slowly made my way along the coast pleased with my timing as I wasn't going to have to lay off and wait for the sun to rise before coming in. My intention was to grab a mooring ball for the night and ring in the New Year on the island before making my way home on the first day of the New Year. If the mooring fields were sold out due to the holiday, I would drop the hook for the night.

As I motored into the cove at 7:30 am, I was amazed at how empty the anchorage was. It was almost completely empty. Back in my regular stomping grounds, I was soon approaching my assigned mooring, Kilo 4, and my solo adventure to Santa Cruz Island had officially come to an end.

- Sailor James

POSITION LOG:

13:00 – 34°02'80"N 119°32'76"W
Departed

00:00 – 33°44'89"N 118°58'06"W
Underway

06:00 – 33°30'59"N 118°33'78"W
Underway

07:30 – 33°26'53"N 118°29'81"W
Tied up to Mooring K4
Two Harbors, Isthmus Cove

LOG NOTES:

*Heavy Fog until sunset
*Autotiller worked out (on reverse settings)
*Engine did great
*Fog throughout the night
*Dolphins throughout the night
*Easy peaceful passage

- The Last Weighing of Anchor on Santa Cruz Island -

- Sailing into the Fog -

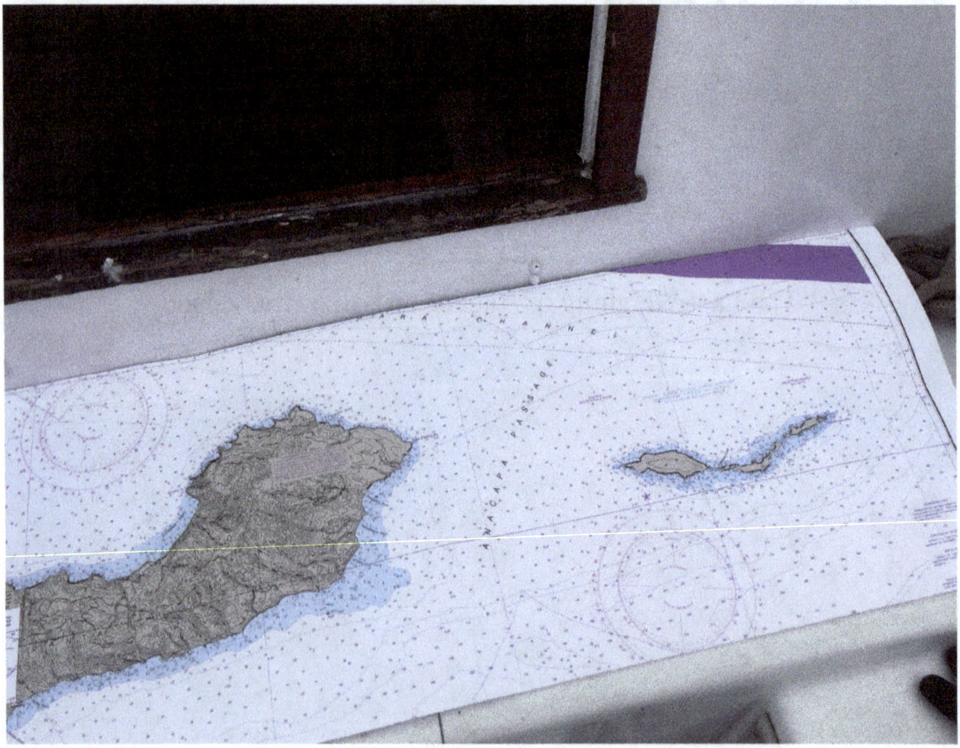

- Just Say Yes to Paper Charts -

- Sailing into the Fog -

- Anacapa -

- Silence, Sailing and Magic Hour -

- Silence, Sailing and Magic Hour -

- Shiprock Light at Sunrise -

- Shiprock -

- Two Harbors, Catalina Island -

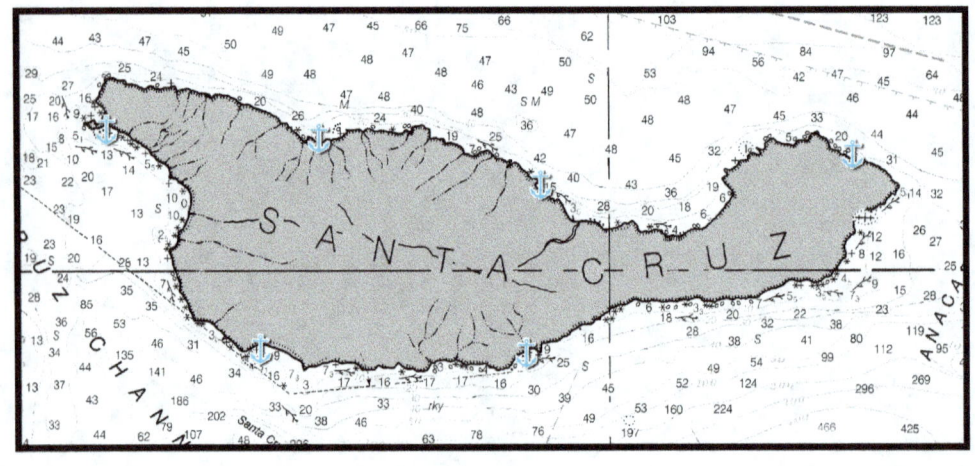

Coches Prietos
33°58'05"N 119°42'25"W

Morse Point
33°57'54"N 119°50'34"W

Forney Cove
34°03'23"N 119°55'13"W

Cueva Valdez
34°03'10"N 119°49'03"W

Pelican Bay
34°02'01"N 119°42'08"W

Little Scorpion
34°02'45"N 119°32'43"W

Sailing Vessel Triteia - Sailing to Coches Prietos Anchorage, Santa Cruz Island

17 episodes

Hello Friends, Welcome to A Stern View Podcast! This is a sailing podcast that is meant to be a "Cruisers Guide to Anchorages". I feel there are a lot of great interview based sailing podcasts so I decided to try something different and bring more

A STERN VIEW PODCAST : a sailing podcast

Sailor James

Sports

★★★★★ 4.8, 10 Ratings

Listen on Apple Podcasts ↗

SEP 8, 2019
EP 019: On the Hook At Cabrillo Harbor
In this episode we talk about the amazing anchorage of Cabrillo Harbor at Catalina Island. After an adventurous departure from Button Shell Beach, getting prop'd by our dinghy line and Camille diving to free it. We dropped a stern and bow anchor at Cabrillo Beach in 17 feet of water

▶ PLAY   32 min

AUG 26, 2019
EP 018: Anchoring at Button Shell Beach on Catalina Island
EP018: Anchoring at Button Shell Beach on Catalina Island.

In this episode we talk about our experiences anchoring at Button Shell Beach and Whites Cov

▶ PLAY   29 min

To see video episodes of
the stories you have just read and to
follow along with our
future adventures please visit

YOUTUBE.COM/SAILORJAMES

Also check out my
"a cruising guide to anchorages"
sailing podcast

A STERN VIEW PODCAST

AFT

James Frederick is currently based in Los Angeles and is finishing up the refit on SV Triteia. In the spring of 2020 Frederick and his wife Camille will leave for full-time cruising. The two will continue to make videos and write about their adventures from the Sea of Cortez before heading to Central America and further south to explore the canals of Chile and round Cape Horn.

If you would like to see more about the art he created on the SY Selkie you can visit : huffpost.com/author/jfrede

At the time of this printing Frederick has passed all the necessary tests for his Masters Captains 50-ton License with plans to work as a delivery captain to fund their cruising.

svtriteia.com

notes:

notes:

www.ingramcontent.com/pod-product-compliance
Lightning Source LLC
Chambersburg PA
CBHW050557300426
44112CB00013B/1959